FORTY TRUMPET PLAYER DUETS

FORTY
TRUMPET
PLAYER
DUETS
Eddie Lewis

Published 2023 by
Edward Lewis
A division of Tiger Music
Houston, Texas, 77089.

Cover art by Pearl Lewis

Perfect Bound
ISBN 978-0-9818918-9-7

http://www.tigermusicstore.com

Dedication

Trumpet duets are not only an educational tool for trumpet players. There is also a culture of playing duets for fun in the trumpet community. This "trumpet fun time" serves to bring us together in a social setting and I have fond memories of times playing duets with friends over the years. I've been doing it since I was in intermediate school.

This book is dedicated primarily to Fred Easter, a current adult student of mine. Fred has read through all these duets with me in his recent lessons, which has helped me greatly with the editing process. Private lessons are not necessarily "trumpet fun time", but sometimes duets are necessary for the students' growth. And who says you can't have a bit of fun in your trumpet lessons?

I also want to dedicate this book to every trumpet player I ever played duets with. These include past classmates, past teachers, many of my own students and fellow professionals. None of us play duets as often as we would like, and it becomes even more difficult to pull it off as we age, but as far as I know, we all enjoy our time making music this way.

So, thank all of you for your time and enthusiasm. Each of you has played a role in shaping this **Forty Trumpet Player Duets** book.

Table of Contents

Introduction

Here we are with book number three in our trumpet duet series. We began with **Twenty Trumpet Pioneer Duets**, then we published **Twenty Trumpet Tyro Duets** soon afterwards. Both of those were beginner trumpet duet books. This third book, **Forty Trumpet Player Duets,** is a duet book for intermediate trumpet students.

There are two intermediate levels in our system, and the Trumpet Player level is the first of those two.

I have been composing trumpet duets my entire life. I began writing duets when I was in seventh grade, living in Hawaii (I went to Wahiawa Intermediate School on the island of Oahu). I have written hundreds of trumpet duets since seventh grade, and I **love** it! I always have.

This book, **Forty Trumpet Player Duets,** is our sixth duet book. We started with **Celebrations: 101 Original Trumpet Duets**. **Celebrations** is a book for all skill levels, starting with beginner duets and progressing gradually towards trumpet duets that would give the most seasoned professional a challenge.

The next trumpet duet book we published was **Trumpet Hymn Duets**, which has become one of our best-selling books. Then there were the two earlier books in this series, mentioned in the first paragraph. Most recently we published our **Trumpet Christmas Duets** book.

> **I have written hundreds of trumpet duets since seventh grade, and I love it! I always have.**

To me, these duets are all real pieces of music. That is why I enjoy writing them so much. It is also why so many trumpet players enjoy playing them. These trumpet duets can and should be used educationally, but the duets themselves are not dummied down. They are truly expressive works of art, created with specific parameters. Those parameters are determined by the skill level of the students whom the duets were written.

Writing duets for this series, in graduated skill levels, is like the story of *Goldilocks and the Three Bears*. When I compose duets for these books, I try to create <u>music</u> that is "just right" for that skill level. Which is not always as easy as it might seem.

Celebrations Duets

There is some overlap between this book and the original **Celebrations** duet book. When **Celebrations** was written, print-on-demand technology was not as prominent as it is today. It was a good idea at the time to write one book that trumpet players of all seven levels could play from. This Arban-esque approach (something for everyone) works well when the cost of purchasing and storing huge numbers of books is an obstacle. But with print-on-demand technology, writing and publishing separate books for very specific categories of trumpet players is now not only a workable option, but also a more practical option.

Almost 75% of the duets in this book are brand new.

We can now publish duet books for each skill level in our system. We want you to have a book dedicated entirely to your current needs, at your current skill level.

That said, there are only twelve **Celebrations** duets in this collection of forty trumpet duets. That means almost 75% of the duets in this book are brand new. (We mention this in case you already have the **Celebrations** book.)

Trumpet Player Duets

In the previous two books in this series, I listed the parameters I used to limit my writing for those books. I cannot do the same for this book, because there is more to it than what I can put here in a couple paragraphs.

What I can do is speak generally about these duets. There is a reason why we call this the **Trumpet Player** level. A student who plays at this level can confidently tell people, "Yes, I am a trumpet player." Almost all the elements required to perform ensemble music are already within this student's grasp.

The greatest difference between students at the **Trumpet Player** skill level and more advanced students is how long it takes them to learn a new piece of music. Of course, range is also a factor for many trumpet players. So, in this **Forty Trumpet Player Duets** book, we have fully skilled music with limited range. Nothing in this book goes any higher than G sharp above the staff.

Three Sections

The duets in **Forty Trumpet Player Duets** are grouped into three sections. The first half of the book (section one) is dedicated to tonal music in all twelve key signatures (sometimes major, sometimes minor). The second section includes duets that fall on the more jazzy side of our art. Not all of these are necessarily swing duets, but the rhythms are not strictly classical.

The third section (the last 12 duets) of the book focuses on more modern composition techniques. Most of these duets are "atonal" in the sense that they do not have tonal centers, but they are not nearly as dissonant as what we usually expect from "atonal" compositions. I call these my "experimental" compositions, because they evolved through a process of experimentation.

Comprehensive Keys

I invested a lot of effort to make sure all the key signatures were appropriately represented. To reach that objective, I have multiple versions of several of the duets. They are transposed to a variety of keys so you have the opportunity to read real music in each of those keys.

Proficient reading in all keys is an important part of my teaching system. That's why we recommend that you observe our recommended prerequisites. Read more about the prerequisites in the section titled **Trumpet Player Tonalization Studies**.

Assignments vs. Sight-Reading

The skill level of the duets in the book makes them appropriate for Trumpet Player Students to use as assignments, but not for sight-reading. These duets are designed to be at the proper level for intermediate students to use as practicing material. In contrast, all sight-reading materials should be at least one skill level easier than the student's current skill level.

If you, as an intermediate player, want a duet book for sight-reading, then we suggest the **Twenty Trumpet Tyro Duets** book for that.

The **Forty Trumpet Player Duets** book should be used as sight-reading materials for students at the **Trumpet Apprentice** level or higher.

Trumpet Player Tonalization Studies

It should be every musician's goal to read all keys equally well. The only reason we don't is because we rarely spend enough time practicing and performing in the less common keys. We are unfamiliar with the so called "hard keys", and then we stumble when those keys pop up in our parts.

If you are using this duet book as part of my full system, then it is important to only practice or sight-read the duets in keys for which you have already done the Tonalization Studies. Reading and practicing music in an ensemble setting is the last step in the Tonalization system.

When you follow my method, your key signature progress should conform to the following order:

1. Do the **Major Scale Expansion Studies** for a new key. (See the **Major Scale Expansion Studies** eBook for those exercises available as a PDF download at TigerMusicStore.com.)
2. Practice the **Trumpet Player Tonalization Studies** in that key at least ten times.
3. Sight-read or practice songs or etudes in that key.
4. Sight-read or practice ensemble music in that key.

In my system, trumpet duets are considered ensemble music.

> **It should be every musician's goal to read all keys equally well.**

If you are unaware of my system, then I would encourage you to purchase two of the books that support the learning of the duets in the **Forty Trumpet Player Duets** book. They are: **Trumpet Major Scale Expansion Studies** and **Total Tonalization**.

For noting: **Total Tonalization** will eventually be republished under the title, **Trumpet Player Tonalization Studies**, to match the other books in the Tonalization series. Currently, the book is still being published under the title **Total Tonalization**.

If you do not use my Tonalization system, then **Forty Trumpet Player Duets** works equally well as a normal duet book. There is no need to pursue other supporting books if you are not following my system.

Dynamic Convention

The dynamic convention I follow in **Forty Trumpet Player Duets** is modeled on some of the older, classic duet book staples. Duet books that I have in my library which follow this convention include books by:

- Arthur Amsden
- Joseph Forestier
- Domenico Gatti
- Sigmund Hering
- Bob Nelson
- H. A. Vander Cook
- H. Voxman

More modern books from my library that also follow this convention include duet books by:

- Ken Davies
- Ellen Levy-Ryan
- Etienne Ozi

What is this convention and how does it differ from today's publishing?

In most classic trumpet duet books, the dynamics (and some other markings) are placed between the two staves, for both parts. The only time each part gets its own dynamics is when they have different dynamics. If one part should be *p* and the other *f,* then both parts are marked with their own dynamics. As long as they are both playing the same dynamic, the marking goes between the two parts.

In today's modern publishing, it is more common to see both parts marked with every dynamic, whether they are playing the same dynamic or not.

> **What can I say? I'm a trumpet duet junky!**

I have two stacks of duet books in front of me right now, separated according to this convention. The pile of books that do not follow the convention modeled by the classic trumpet duet books is three times the size of the pile of books that do follow this convention. (Yes, I know that's a LOT of trumpet duet books. What can I say? I'm a trumpet duet junky!)

When I look at the pages of the modern trumpet duet books, the clutter is unsettling.

No Dynamics?

There are many duets in **Forty Trumpet Player Duets** that basically have no dynamics written. I don't believe every piece of music must have dynamic contrast. Sometimes, to insert arbitrary dynamics for no musical reason deters from the music. For these duets, I simply put an *mf* at the beginning which means to play the duet at a comfortable volume.

About the Trumpet Player Level

The method I use to teach my students is divided into seven graduated skill levels. The Trumpet Player level is the third of those seven. Students who graduate from the Trumpet Player level have their proverbial "foot in the door" for most trumpet music. These are students who I no longer consider beginners. They have mastered all twelve major keys. They can read all the most typical time signatures. They can play most standard rhythms and understand basic phrasing. These are students who have breached the beginner threshold and have become genuine Trumpet Players.

My system staggers the development of important trumpet skills evenly over all levels. In that sense, it truly is a journey. The following illustration demonstrates where the Trumpet Player is in that journey. The Trumpet Pioneer is the absolute beginner who lands at Port Bucina on the map. The Trumpet Pioneer graduates from absolute beginner to work in the Tyro Territory. When the Trumpet Tyro graduates, then it's time to work on the Trumpet Player materials. All the ELM territories lead to increasingly better trumpet performance. Where are you on this map?

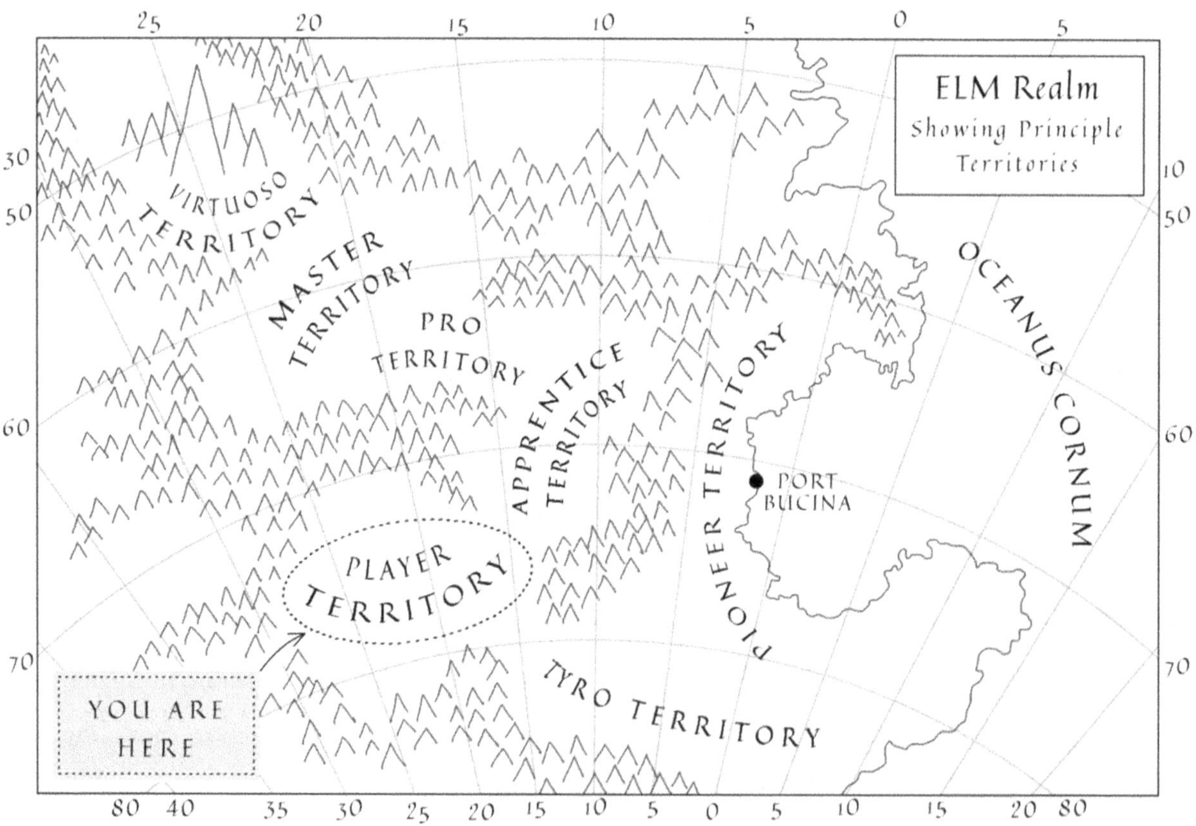

Faith Springs Fanfare

Eddie Lewis

Composed for and performed at the opening of the new
sanctuary building at Faith Springs Baptist Church in 2022.

My Only Love

No. 2

Eddie Lewis

21
f
C
25
p
f
29
f
D
33
p
rit.

Keeping Promises

No. 3

Eddie Lewis

All Day Kisses

Eddie Lewis

No. 4

Hopeful

Eddie Lewis

No. 6
Morning Dance
Eddie Lewis
Light and Fun
mp
mp
mf
A
B
f
Forty Trumpet Player Duets - PG 14

21
C
25
ff
p
D
29
33
rit.
mp

Minor March

Eddie Lewis

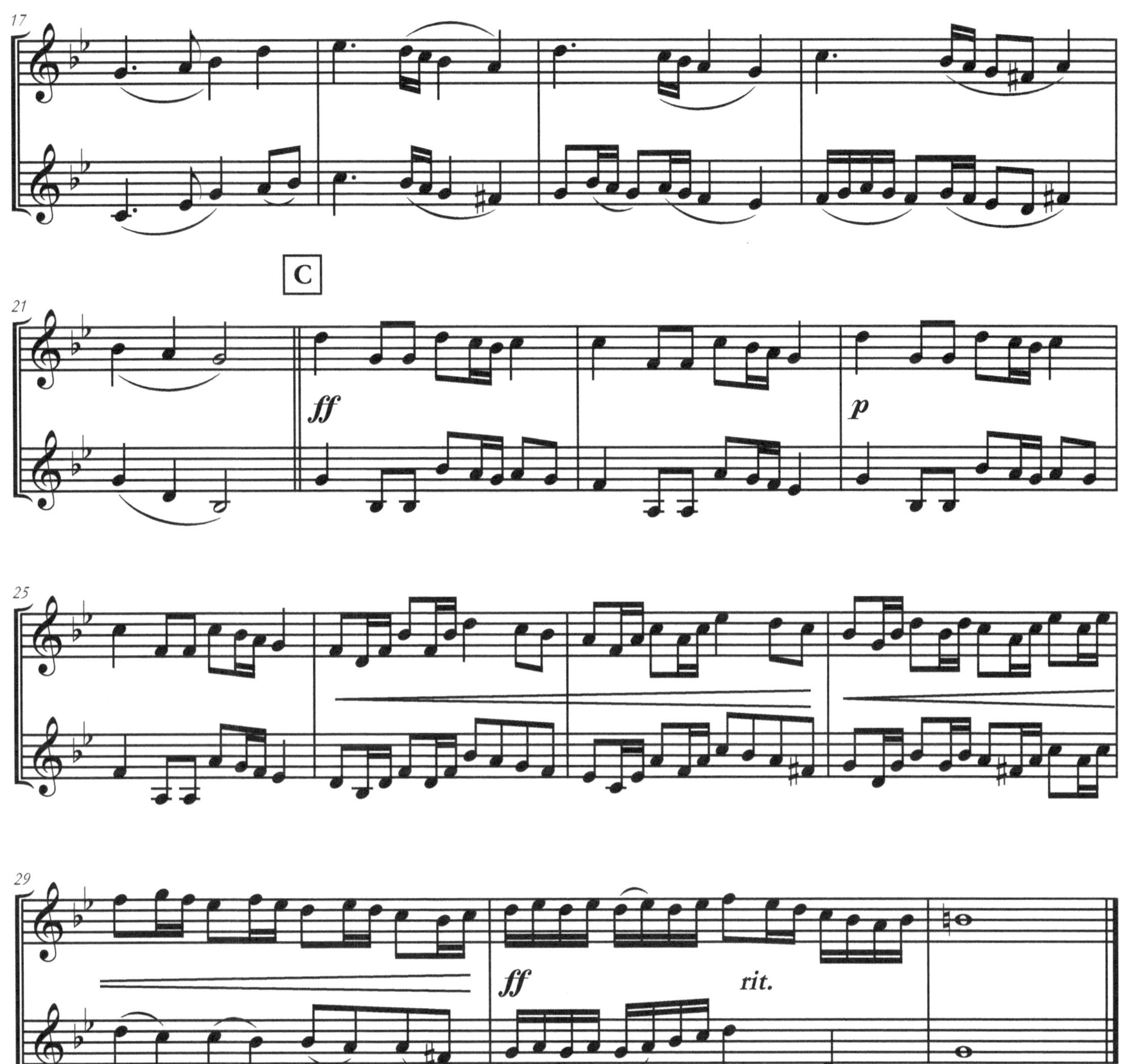
C
ff
p
ff
rit.

Cyclic Delights

No. 8

Eddie Lewis

C
22
f
D
27
32
p
E
36
mf
41

Time After Time

Eddie Lewis

Time After Time

No. 9B

Eddie Lewis

Time After Time

No. 9C

Eddie Lewis

Time After Time

No. 9D

Eddie Lewis

Rain Song

Eddie Lewis

Sherwood Forest

Eddie Lewis

Sherwood Forest

Eddie Lewis

Sherwood Forest

No. 11C

Eddie Lewis

Sherwood Forest

Sherwood Forest

No. 11E

Eddie Lewis

No. 12A — Honest and Simple

Eddie Lewis

Dedicated to Marcel Boily

Honest and Simple

Eddie Lewis

Dedicated to Marcel Boily

No. 12C
Honest and Simple
Eddie Lewis
Dedicated to Marcel Boily
Dolce ♩= 120
mf
1.
2.
K
f
mf
mp
L
p
f
mf
mp
Forty Trumpet Player Duets - PG 34

Honest and Simple

Honest and Simple

No. 12E

Eddie Lewis

Dedicated to Marcel Boily

Honest and Simple

Eddie Lewis

Dedicated to Marcel Boily

Uninspired

Uninspired

Eddie Lewis

Uninspired

190
196
203
I
f
211
218
mf
p
mf
rit.

Uninspired

No. 13D

Waltz ♩ = 128

Eddie Lewis

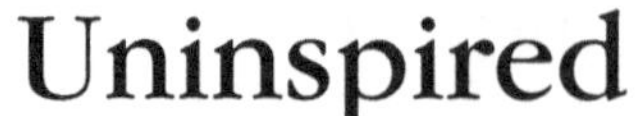

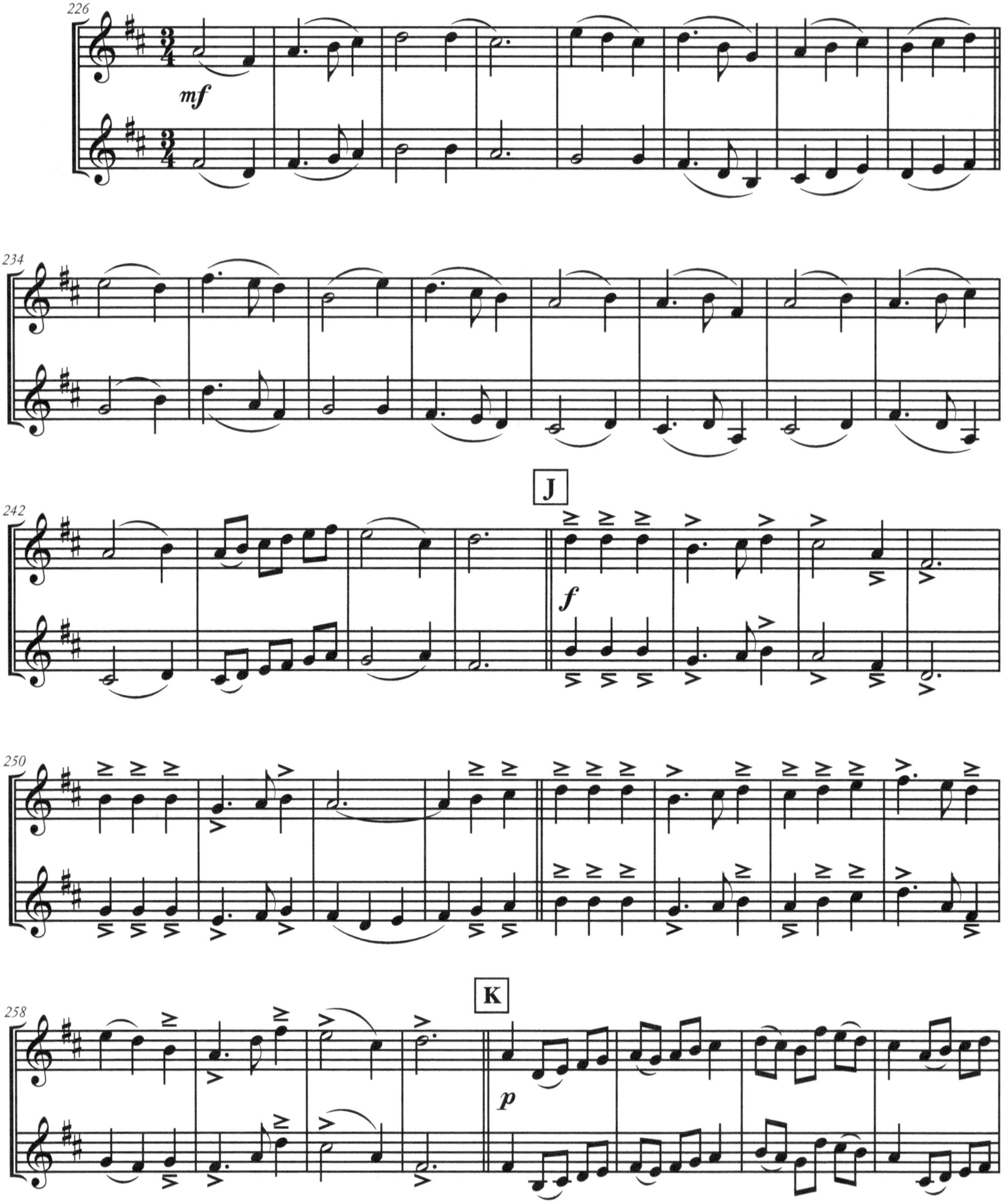

Uninspired

342
349
O
356
f
p
mf
363
370
mf
rit.

Uninspired

No. 13F

418
424
R
432
439
446
mf
p
f
mf
rit.

Origami Organum Outbursts

No. 14

Eddie Lewis

D
E Slower
F
G Tempo 1
rit.

Morning Reign

No. 15

Eddie Lewis

D
Pesante
f
E
Lament
mf
F

A Theme for Gardeners

No. 16

Eddie Lewis

rit.
C
a tempo

D
42
46
rit.

Riverboat Adrift

No. 17

Eddie Lewis

I Will Sing Tomorrow

C
D
f

I Will Sing Tomorrow

F
54
57
G
60
f
65
H
70

I Will Sing Tomorrow

No. 18C

Eddie Lewis

Remember When?

Eddie Lewis

32
poco a poco cresc....
D
36
f
40
3
3
3
E
44
mp
50

Remember When?

No. 19B

Eddie Lewis

poco a poco cresc....
I
f
3
3
3
J
mp

Remember When?

No. 19C

Eddie Lewis

139
poco a poco cresc....
N
143
f
146
3
3
3
O
150
mp
156

Hacerlo Rey

No. 20

Eddie Lewis

C
D

No. 21
Comin' Home
Remenbering Keith Anderson
Eddie Lewis
Gospel
mf
A
B

Resulting Bliss

No. 22

Eddie Lewis

C
D
E

No. 23 — Paid to Play

Eddie Lewis

45
D
49
f
53
58
63

E
67
72
77
82

Picking Oranges

No. 24

Eddie Lewis

No. 25

Fancy Dance

Eddie Lewis

Swing ♩ = 160

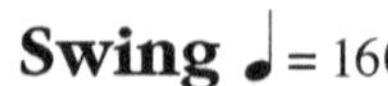

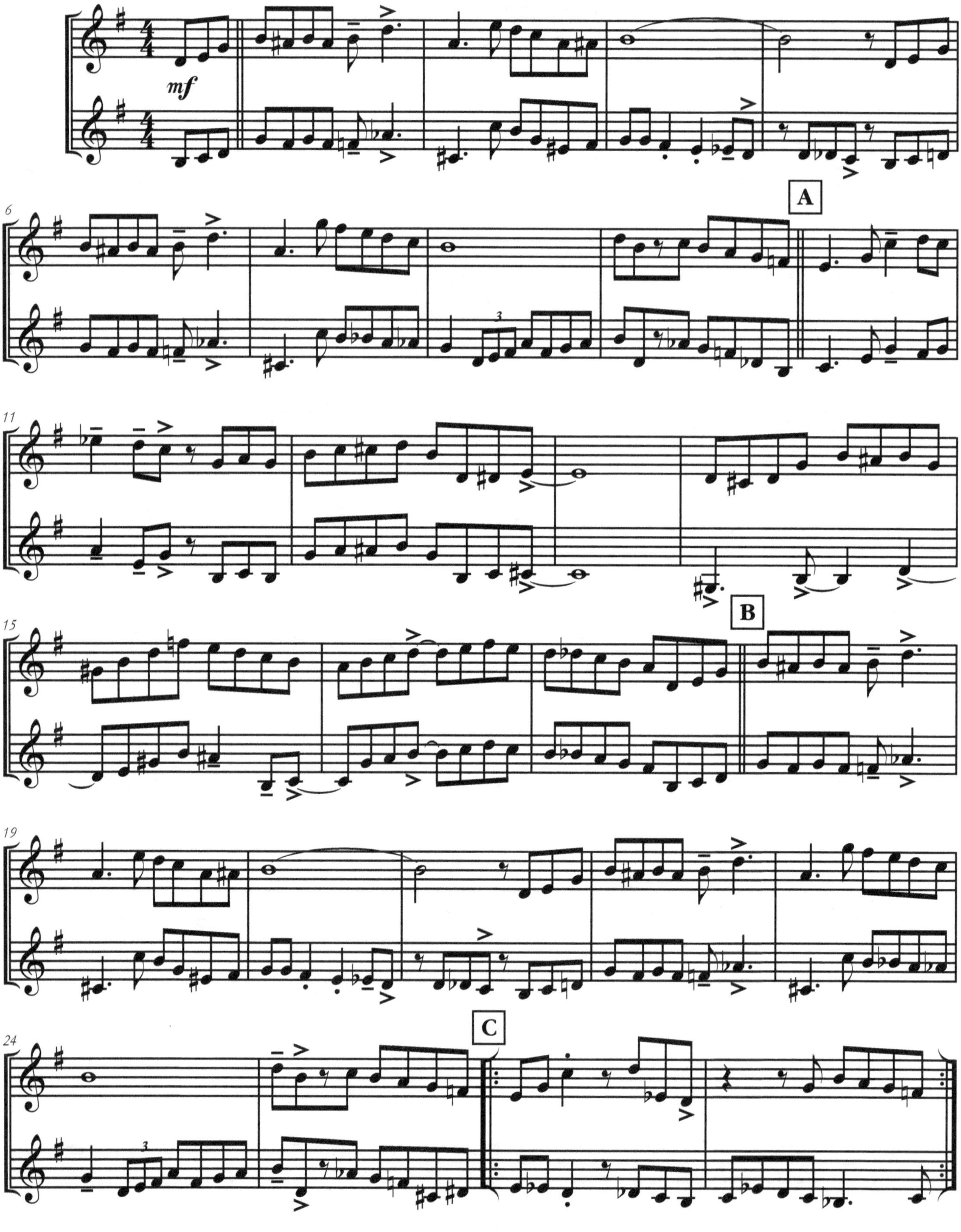

When the Saints Go Marching In

Arr. Eddie Lewis

B

Straight
C
Straight
Straight
Straight
Straight

Hermit's Dance Supreme!

No. 27

Eddie Lewis

20
B Slower ♩= 69
mp
mf
f
24
mf
mp   rit.
28
32
poco a poco accel.
C Tempo I ♩= 100
mf
35
39

Banzai Bravery

C
fp ff p
D
mf
rit.

No. 29A — Joy, Joy, Everyone Is Flying

Eddie Lewis

* First two measures in first part are optional.

Joy, Joy, Everyone Is Flying

Eddie Lewis

* First two measures in first part are optional.

Joy, Joy, Everyone Is Flying

Eddie Lewis

* First two measures in first part are optional.

Let All Mortal Flesh

Christina G. Rossetti, Gustav T. Holst
Arr. Eddie Lewis

31
37
43
accel.
Faster ♩ = 96
49
f
54

60
65
Adagio ♩ = 69
rit.
mf
71
rit.
76

Brady Bird

No. 31

Critter Suite Movement One

Eddie Lewis

Vladdie Mouse
Critter Suite Movement Two

No. 32

Eddie Lewis

Siggie Bear

No. 33

Critter Suite Movement Three

Eddie Lewis

L
110
113
M
115
dim.
118
rit.

Dorrie Deer

No. 34

Critter Suite Movement Four

Eddie Lewis

Spider Twins

No. 35

Eddie Lewis

Reverent Spider

Original Prime

Eddie Lewis

C
25
D
30
35
rit.

Left Out Version Eight

No. 38

Eddie Lewis

C
mf
rit.
D
p
accel.
rit.
ff

Machinations

Webster's dictionary defines machination as *"a scheming or crafty action or artful design intended to accomplish some usually evil end"*. The older I get; the more life seems to become a gauntlet of plots against me. I'm sure I'm not alone in this, so the last two trumpet duets in this book are meant to express a resolve and commitment to finish strong. Whatever this evil world throws our way, we are going to endure. We are going to strive. We are going to win.

"11 Put on the whole armour of God, that ye may be able to stand against the wiles of the devil. 12 For we wrestle not against flesh and blood, but against principalities, against powers, against the rulers of the darkness of this world, against spiritual wickedness in high places." **Ephesians 6:11-12**

Technically, Machinations falls slightly outside of the Trumpet Player skill level. I chose to include it anyway because it was only on one point that the piece went "out of bounds". The range is limited to G and there is nothing in the piece that a student at the Trumpet Player level cannot master (given enough practice time). So I decided to keep it as something of an introduction to the next duet book in the series.

Many of the duets in the Forty Trumpet Player Duets book have interesting background stories like the explanation offered above. If you would like to read more of these, then I encourage you to look for the individual duets on our website, TigerMusicStore.com. We are in the process of adding the individual duets to our online inventory and many of those pages will have similar back stories.

Prelude to Machination

Eddie Lewis

Machination

No. 40

Eddie Lewis

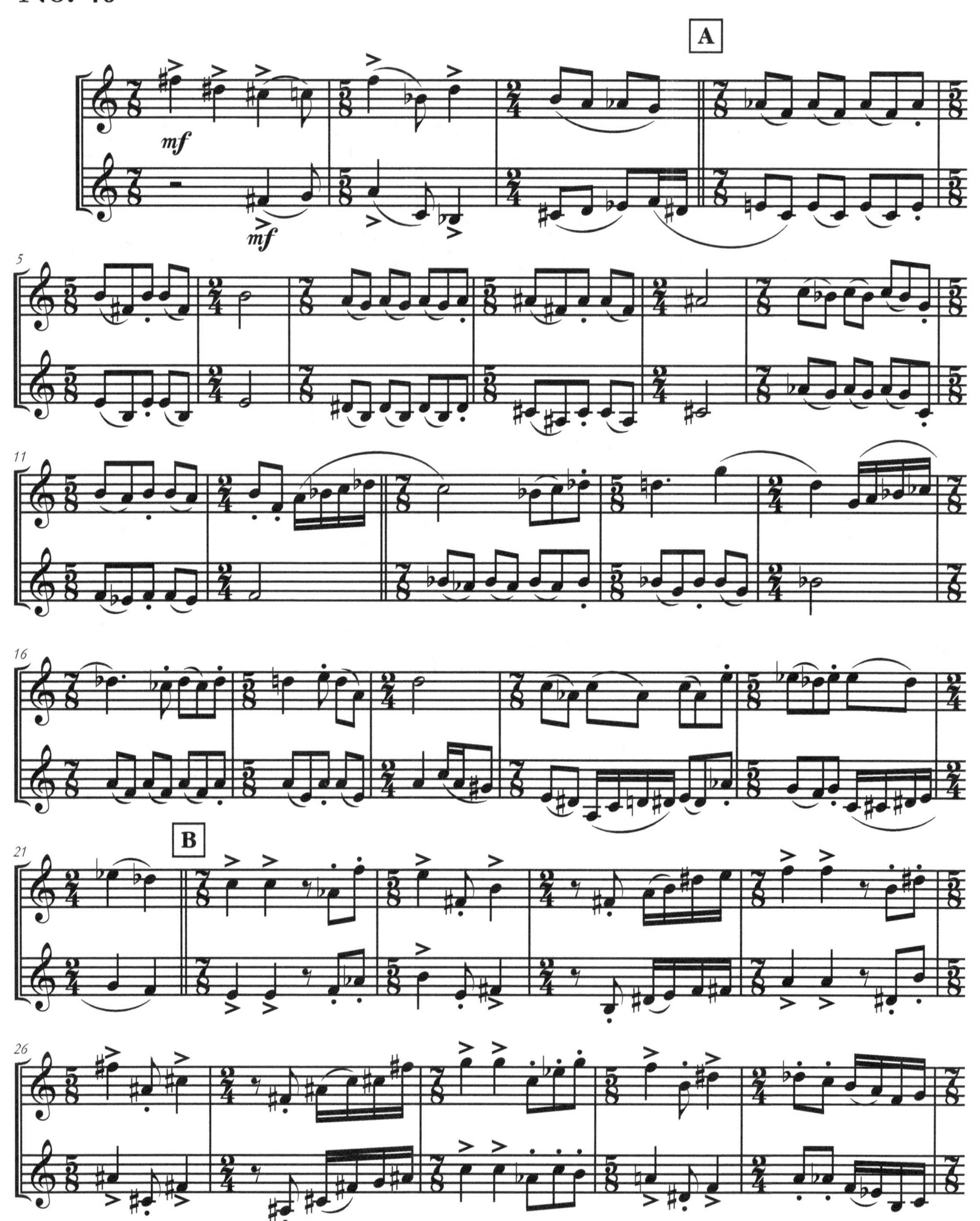

C
a tempo
rit.
D
E
rit.

Eddie Lewis

Sharing What Works

Eddie Lewis has been teaching trumpet lessons since 1980 when he was a junior at Andress High School, in El Paso, Texas. He has always had a passion for sharing what he knows. You can call it teaching, but it's a very specific style of teaching – a style which implies that the teacher has knowledge and experience to share. In Eddie Lewis' case, this experience includes decades as a full-time, performing musician and successful private lesson teacher.

One of Eddie Lewis' most important qualities as a teacher is that he has a solid foundation in traditional, academic pedagogy. Even though some of what he teaches seems almost revolutionary, it is all grounded in tradition. For almost two decades Eddie studied with seven different, long-term trumpet teachers. When he took his education forward into a full-time performance career, covering all genres applicable to the trumpet, it gave him a practical environment in which to test those traditions. Some of the accepted conventions did not survive the test. In those few areas where the traditions fell short, Eddie's new methods took root.

You might not have heard of Eddie Lewis. He's not a famous musician, nor a famous teacher. People study with Eddie and buy his books, not because of who he is, but because his approach works. His methods for physical brass rudiments, jazz improvisation, literature preparation, and performance anxiety have been proven successful by his students and the thousands of musicians who he has helped through his books, websites and articles.